Discover and Do!

LIGHT

GET HANDS-ON WITH SCIENCE

Written by Jane Lacey

W

FRANKLIN WATTS

Franklin Watts
First published in Great Britain in 2021
by The Watts Publishing Group
Copyright © The Watts Publishing Group, 2021

Produced for Franklin Watts by
White-Thomson Publishing Ltd
www.wtpub.co.uk

HB ISBN: 978 1 4451 7723 6
PB ISBN: 978 1 4451 7741 0

Editor: Katie Dicker
Designer: Clare Nicholas
Series designer: Rocket Design (East Anglia) Ltd

Picture credits:
t=top b=bottom m=middle l=left r=right

Shutterstock: La Gorda *cover/title page l*, MaryDesy *cover/title page r*, 4, 10b and 31b, Anatolir 5tl and 7tr, Ara Hovhannisyan 5br and 8m, Diki Prayogo 6t, Maurice Tricatelle 8b, Sonya illustration 12, Blablo101 14tr and 29tr, vectorpouch 14m, Lina Truman 15tr, OnD 15tr, baldezh 16b, GoodStudio 16br, equinoxvect 18b, Bukavik 18br, Kateryna Lomakina 20tr, Maha Heang 245789 20b, Flat vectors 23tr and 30b, diluck 24l and 31m, Ebichan 24br, Phovoir 25tr, Oceloti 26tr and 28, Ann in the uk 26b; Getty: anuwat meereewee 5tr, 18tl and 30t, vectortatu 6b, Kerkez 7m, FORGEM 7b, Xurzon 10tl and 32, Macrovector 14b and 29br, kertlis 16tr, OGI75 19tr, Bigmouse108 20br, hekakoskinen 20bl, zvukmedia 22tr, artcyclone 22b, Anastasiia_M 27tr and 31t.

All design elements from Shutterstock.
Craft models from a previous series by Q2AMedia.

Every attempt has been made to clear copyright. Should there be any inadvertent omission, please apply to the publisher for rectification.

Printed in China

Franklin Watts
An imprint of
Hachette Children's Group
Part of The Watts Publishing Group
Carmelite House
50 Victoria Embankment
London EC4Y 0DZ

An Hachette UK Company
www.hachettechildrens.co.uk

DISCOVER AND DO!

LIGHT

GET HANDS-ON WITH SCIENCE

W
FRANKLIN WATTS
LONDON•SYDNEY

CONTENTS

Words that appear in **bold** can be found in the glossary on pages 28–29.

WHAT IS LIGHT?

Light is a kind of **energy**. The Sun is the greatest source of natural light on Earth. Our eyes need light to see, so when the Sun goes down at night, we turn on lights or burn candles to see.

Travelling light

Light travels in a straight line at 300,000 kilometres a second. It is the fastest moving thing in the universe! Light from the Sun takes about 8 minutes 20 seconds to travel through space to Earth. You must never look directly at the Sun. It is too bright for our eyes.

At night, we use **artificial** light to help us to see.

The Sun gives out the heat and light energy that all life on Earth needs to survive.

Luminous

Things that give out light are **luminous**. Some luminous things give out brighter, more intense light than others. The brightness of car headlights is more intense than the brightness of candlelight, for example.

This torch is luminous. It gives out a beam of light to read by.

Moonlight is pale because it is **reflected** light from the Sun.

Reflected light

We see some objects when light bounces off them, or is reflected into our eyes. The Moon is not luminous so it does not give out light. We see the Moon when the Sun shines on it. The Moon reflects sunlight into our eyes.

WHAT IS DARK?

Where there is no light, it is dark. It is dark wherever light cannot reach – in your bedroom when you turn out the light and close the curtains, or at the bottom of the sea and in deep caves, for example.

Day and night

Earth takes 24 hours to spin around once in space. It is night when the half of Earth you are on is turning away from the Sun. It is day when your half of Earth is facing the Sun.

day

Sun's rays

night

Earth turns every 24 hours. It is day for the half facing the Sun, and night for the half facing away from the Sun.

Living in the dark

Some animals, such as owls, have large eyes to help them see in the dark. Other animals use their senses of smell and touch in the darkness. Some deep-sea fish and night insects make their own light and glow in the dark to attract prey or find a mate.

Glow-worms give out a green glow or a flashing light to attract a mate in the dark.

MAKE A MODEL EARTH

Ask an adult to help you with this activity

You will need:
- **bowl and spoon**
- **water**
- **flour**
- **salt**
- **scales**
- **round balloon**
- **newspaper**
- **straight stick about 50 cm long**
- **pen and paints**
- **atlas**
- **torch**

1 In a bowl, stir 375 ml of water, 75 grams of flour and 7 grams of salt together to make a smooth paste like glue.

2 Blow up the balloon and tie the end securely. Tear strips of newspaper about 6 cm by 3 cm and dip them into the paste.

3 Stick the strips onto the balloon in layers to make a round ball-shaped 'Earth'. Leave to dry. When the paper is dry, ask an adult to help you pop the balloon and push the stick carefully through the centre of the ball and out the other side.

4 Paint the ball to look like Earth, with the stick going through the north and south pole. Use an atlas to find where you are on Earth and mark this position on your planet.

5 In a darkened room, hold your model Earth in a beam of torchlight. Gradually turn the stick and watch your part of Earth move from day to night.

LIGHT RAYS

Light travels away from a light source in straight lines called **rays**. Sometimes you can see rays of light from the Sun shining through trees, from behind clouds or through a window.

Lighting up the dark

Rays from a strong light source, such as the Sun, travel long distances and light up a large area. Rays from a weaker source, such as a candle, travel shorter distances and light up a small area.

Rays of sunlight are shining through gaps between the trees in this forest.

One direction

Light can only travel in straight lines (or beams). You can clearly see the straight, narrow beam of a torch or car headlight in the dark, for example. A theatre spotlight sends out a beam of light to show a dancer on the stage, leaving the rest of the theatre in darkness.

A lighthouse sweeps a beam of light across the water to warn ships at night of dangerous rocks.

HIT THE TARGET!

Ask an adult to help you with this activity

You will need:
- **1 square of paper and 5 squares of strong card (15 cm x 15 cm)**
- **scissors**
- **pencil and paints (or coloured pens)**
- **modelling clay**
- **ruler**
- **torch**

1 Fold the paper in half both ways to find the centre point. Open it out and put it on top of four of the card squares.

2 Ask an adult to push sharp scissors through the centre of the four pieces of card, using the paper as a guide. Cut a small circle around each hole. Leave the fifth card uncut – this will be your target. Draw a target around the centre.

3 Push each piece of card into a ball of modelling clay (for a stand). Line them up on a table or on the floor about 20 cm apart, with the target at one end of the line. Shine the torch beam through the hole at the other end of the line. Can you line up the holes so the beam of light shines through them and hits the target?

SHADOWS

Light cannot go around corners. When something solid gets in the way of light rays, light cannot shine through it or go around it. This creates a **shadow** that is shaped like the solid object.

Different shadows

As Earth turns around, the Sun seems to move across the sky. In the morning and evening, when the Sun is low in the sky, your shadow is longer than you are. At midday, when the Sun is overhead, your shadow is shorter.

Solid objects have a shadow that is a similar shape to it.

ACTIVITY

MAKE A SUNDIAL

Ask an adult to help you with this activity

You will need:
- **strong, thick A3 card**
- **length of dowel (thin rod of wood), about 25 cm**
- **sticky tape or glue**
- **compass**
- **ruler**
- **waterproof marker pen**
- **waterproof paints**

1 Ask an adult to make a hole in the card, half-way down one of the long sides, about 2 cm from the edge.

2 Push the dowel into the hole so the base of the dowel is level with the underside of the card. Tape or glue it in place so it stands upright. Alternatively, place the sundial on some grass and push the dowel through the hole into the grass to secure it.

3 Use a compass to place the sundial so the stick edge of the card is facing south.

Stick edge

4 On a sunny day, on every hour, with your ruler and marker pen draw a line along the shadow made by the stick. Write the time on each line – 9.00, 10.00, 11.00, etc., and paint each segment.

5 Put your sundial in the same place to tell the time on sunny days. The shadow will move throughout the day as the position of the Sun changes.

SHINING THROUGH

Light can shine through **transparent materials**. Glass, clear plastic and clean water are transparent – you can see through them. Light cannot shine through **opaque** materials such as wood, metal and card.

Sunglasses have a tinted **lens** to protect your eyes from bright sunlight.

Translucent

Some materials are **translucent**, which means some light can pass through them. Sunglasses are translucent. They help to protect your eyes from harmful Sun rays. Tracing paper and tissue paper are both translucent materials. When you look through them you can see some light, but only blurred shapes.

The glass of this fish tank is transparent, while the plastic casing is opaque.

Materials

Materials are often chosen because of the way light shines through them. Glass, for example, is transparent. Glass windows let you see in and out. Thick bedroom curtains are opaque. They keep out the light to help you sleep.

You can clearly see how much water is in a glass beaker (left). Plastic beakers let less light through them.

ACTIVITY

MAKE A LIGHT AND SHADOWS COLLAGE

You will need:
- **selection of paper (e.g. white paper, coloured tissue paper, tracing paper)**
- **foil**
- **thin card**
- **thin white cotton material**
- **scissors**
- **sheet of clear plastic (A3)**
- **glue**
- **powerful torch**

2 Try to guess which materials will let light through. Make a chart to show your guesses.

3 In a dark room, shine the torch through the plastic sheet onto a white wall. How good were your guesses? What do you notice about the shadows?

1 Cut different shapes from the paper, foil, card and cotton. Stick them onto one side of the clear plastic sheet to make a picture.

REFLECTION

When rays of light hit something, they bounce off it, like a ball bouncing off a hard surface. This is called reflection. Different surfaces cause the light rays to reflect in different ways.

The reflection in this water becomes blurred when light bounces off the ripples in different directions.

Smooth and rough

When light hits a smooth surface, such as flat water in a pond, it bounces off in one direction and you see a reflection. Light bounces off rough, uneven surfaces in all directions. You don't see a clear reflection in a choppy sea, for example.

Mirrors

Mirrors are made of smooth glass covering a layer of shiny metal. When light rays hit the mirror, they bounce straight back and you see your reflection.

You can see your reflection in a flat, shiny mirror.

MAKE A KALEIDOSCOPE

You will need:
- **3 rectangles of foil card, all the same size (about 20 cm x 5 cm) or very shiny foil glued onto card**
- **sticky tape**
- **pencil**
- **white paper**
- **scissors**
- **coloured paper shapes or metallic confetti**
- **plastic food wrap**

1 Tape the foil card rectangles together to make a triangular **prism** with the shiny side facing inwards.

2 Draw around the triangular end onto the white paper and cut out the triangle shape. Stick the paper triangle to one end of the prism.

Drop the coloured paper shapes (or confetti) into the prism and seal the open end of your kaleidoscope with plastic food wrap.

3 Hold your kaleidoscope up to the light and look through the plastic wrap. You will see a repeated pattern of coloured shapes. Shake the kaleidoscope to change the pattern.

Light from the coloured shapes bounces from mirror to mirror and you see several reflections that make repeated patterns.

REFRACTION

Light travels through water and glass more slowly than it travels through air. When light passes from glass or water to the surrounding air, the rays slightly change direction and bend. This is called **refraction**.

This pencil seems to bend because light rays from the pencil change direction as they leave the water.

Bending light

Refraction makes straight objects, such as a pencil or a canoe paddle, look bent when they are half in and half out of water. This is because light changes direction as it moves from water to air.

Apparent position of fish

Light is refracted as it leaves the water.

It's difficult to catch a fish because it looks closer to the surface than it actually is.

Actual position of fish

Bending shapes

If you look through a big raindrop on a windowpane, the objects you see through the glass will appear to have strange shapes. This is because rays of light bend as they travel through the glass and the water, and change the shape of the things you see.

You see distorted shapes through the raindrops on a window because the light rays are refracted.

ACTIVITY

USE REFRACTION FOR A MAGIC TRICK!

You will need:
- **bowl**
- **coin**
- **modelling clay**
- **jug of water**

1 Place the bowl on a table. Fix a coin to the bottom near side of the bowl with modelling clay.

2 Ask a friend to look at the coin and then move slowly backwards and stop when the coin disappears from view.

3 Pour some water into the bowl. Your friend will be amazed to see the coin reappear!

Light reflected from the coin is bent as it leaves the water and goes into the air, helping your friend to see the coin again.

BIGGER AND SMALLER

Lenses are pieces of curved glass or other transparent material, such as plastic. They refract light rays shining through them and cause them to change direction.

convex lens

light rays

concave lens

Convex lenses refract light rays inwards and concave lenses refract light rays outwards.

Concave and convex

Lenses in glasses help to focus images onto the back of our eyes (see page 25). **Convex lenses** help long-sighted people who cannot see near things clearly. **Concave lenses** help short-sighted people who cannot see distant things well.

Microscope

A **microscope** uses convex lenses to make tiny things look thousands of times bigger than they really are. Light is reflected off a mirror onto the **sample** and through a series of lenses to reach our eyes.

We use a microscope to look at tiny objects such as plant cells (left).

MAKE A MICROSCOPE

Ask an adult to help you with this activity

You will need:
- **clear plastic bottle**
- **scissors**
- **small mirror**
- **modelling clay**
- **cup of water**
- **human hair**

1 Ask an adult to help you cut the top off the bottle. Then cut two narrow vertical strips out of opposite sides of the bottle, and two short horizontal slits near the top of the bottle in the other two sides (see the template below).

2 Angle the small mirror in the bottom of the bottle to reflect light upwards. Use the modelling clay as a support. Push each end of one of the vertical strips into the small horizontal slits to make a platform.

3 Drip one drop of water onto the platform to form a convex lens. Use the other strip as a slide. Put a hair onto the strip and hold it under the platform. The hair will be magnified by the water drop.

Template
2 strips cut from bottle sides

horizontal slit

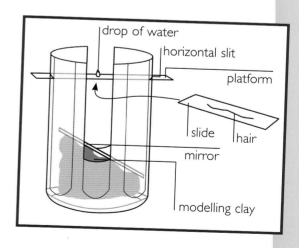

drop of water

horizontal slit

platform

slide

hair

mirror

modelling clay

You can use a **magnifying glass** to make it look even bigger!

DIFFERENT KINDS OF LIGHT

Luminous objects glow in different ways. **Incandescent light** is given out by heat. The Sun gives out incandescent light. When **electricity** passes through older light bulbs, the wire becomes red hot and glows with incandescent light.

This older type of bulb gives out light when the wire becomes hot and glows.

Light in nature

Lightning is a type of natural incandescent light that you see in a storm. During a storm, natural electricity builds up in a cloud and creates a huge spark that we see as a flash of lightning and hear as a crash of thunder.

A flash of lightning lights up the night sky for a few seconds and

Fluorescence

Things that are **fluorescent** do not glow by themselves. They glow in the dark, for example, when light shines on them. Fluorescent strips on clothes glow in the dark when they are caught in the headlights of a car or truck.

Fluorescent strips help to keep you visible and safe when walking at night.

ACTIVITY

MAKE A GLOW IN THE DARK MOBILE

Ask an adult to help you with this activity

You will need:
- **different coloured fluorescent card**
- **pencil**
- **scissors**
- **glue**
- **hole puncher**
- **string**
- **coat hanger**
- **torch**

2 Stick the shapes together so both sides are fluorescent. Punch a hole near the top of each shape and attach different lengths of string.

3 Tie your night-time shapes onto the coat hanger and hang it in your bedroom.

1 Fold the cards in half and draw on night-time shapes such as ghosts, stars, moons and owls. Cut the shapes out of the double card.

4 Test how your mobile glows best – in a completely dark room, in torchlight or in daylight.

SEEING AND LIGHT

We see things around us when light reflects off them into our eyes. It's difficult to see at night when there is only a little light. We see nothing at all in total darkness.

Letting in light

The black circle in the middle of our eyes, called the **pupil**, is a hole that lets in light. The **iris** controls how much light enters our eyes by making the pupil bigger or smaller. This helps our eyes to cope with different strengths of light.

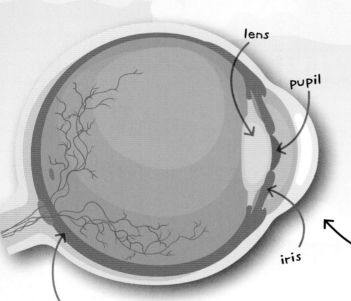

lens

pupil

iris

retina

This diagram shows some of the different parts of our eyes.

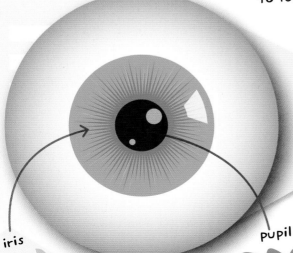

iris

pupil

Your pupils grow large to let in more light. In bright light, they grow smaller to let in less light.

Lenses

Inside our eyes, behind the pupil, is a lens. Reflected light from an object, such as a flower, shines through the pupil onto the lens. The lens focuses this light onto the **retina** and makes an upside-down image of the flower. Our brain turns the image around so we see the flower the right way up.

Light is reflected from this flower into our eyes. The magnifying glass is a lens that makes the flower look bigger.

ACTIVITY

MAKE A CAMERA

Ask an adult to help you with this activity

You will need:
- **small square box without a lid (such as a gift box)**
- **tracing paper**
- **sticky tape**
- **lamp**
- **magnifying glass**

1 Stretch the tracing paper tightly over the open end of the box and tape it in place to make a smooth screen.

2 Ask an adult to make a pinhole in the middle of the opposite side of the box. In a darkened room, point the pinhole at a bright object such as a lamp.

3 Hold the magnifying glass to act as a lens between the lamp and the pinhole. You will see the lamp reflected upside down onto the screen.

Your camera shows how our eyes work. Light enters the small hole (pupil) and shines onto the tracing paper (retina).

COLOURED LIGHT

Light around us seems to be white but, in fact, it is made up of different colours. We only see these colours when light is refracted through something transparent, such as a glass prism.

A glass prism splits white light into the colours of the rainbow.

The spectrum

The colours that make up light are called the **spectrum**. When light shines through a glass prism, the colours travel at different speeds and bend a slightly different amount. The colours separate and we see red, orange, yellow, green, light blue, dark blue and purple.

When sunlight shines through raindrops, they act as tiny prisms and separate the colours of light so we see a rainbow in the sky.

Seeing colours

Our eyes see red, blue and green light. We see the colours of a rainbow when these three colours mix and blend together. A filter is a piece of coloured translucent material, such as glass or tissue paper. A filter only lets light of the same colour through.

We see the different colours of these balloons when mixtures of red, blue and green light are reflected from them.

ACTIVITY

MIX THE COLOURS OF LIGHT

You will need:
- **rectangles of card (70 cm long x 20 cm wide) to make 3 long tubes**
- **sticky tape**
- **3 torches**
- **red, blue and green tissue paper (or cellophane)**
- **large sheet of white paper**

1 Roll each piece of card lengthwise to make tubes that will fit snugly around the ends of the torches. Tape the long edges together.

2 Tape a tube to the end of each torch and tape a piece of coloured tissue paper over the end of each tube.

3 In a dark room, shine the torches onto the white paper and experiment by mixing the three colours of light.

What different colours can you make?

Glossary

artificial

When something is artificial it is man-made rather than natural.

concave lenses

Concave lenses are curved inwards in the middle. They refract light rays outwards.

convex lenses

Convex lenses are curved outwards in the middle. They refract light rays inwards.

electricity

Electricity is a type of energy. We use it to power lights and machines.

energy

Energy is the power that makes things work.

fluorescent

Things that are fluorescent glow in the dark when light shines on them.

incandescent light

Hot objects give out incandescent light. The light from a fire is incandescent.

iris

Your iris is the part of your eye that makes your pupil bigger or smaller to let more or less light through.

lens

A lens is a curved piece of glass or other transparent material that causes light rays to change direction.

luminous

Things that give out light are luminous. The Sun, a torch and a candle are all luminous.

magnifying glass

A magnifying glass is a lens used to make objects look bigger.

materials

Materials are what things are made of. For example, a book is made of paper and a jumper is made of wool.

microscope

A microscope is a piece of equipment that uses lenses to make tiny objects look bigger.

opaque

You cannot see through things that are opaque and light cannot shine through them.

prism

A prism is a solid shape with three flat sides.

pupil

Your pupil is the black circle in the centre of your eye. It is the opening that lets light into your eye.

ray

A ray is a narrow beam of light.

reflected

When light is reflected, it bounces off a surface.

refraction

Refraction is the slight bend in light rays when they pass between air and other transparent materials.

retina

The retina is at the back of your eye. It receives images from the lens and sends them to your brain.

sample

A sample is a small part of something used in a test. A sample of hair can be looked at under a microscope, for example.

shadow

A shadow is a dark shape caused by something coming between rays of light and a surface.

spectrum

The spectrum is all the colours of light. We see the spectrum when sunlight shines through raindrops and a rainbow appears in the sky.

translucent

Translucent materials only let some light shine through them. We cannot see clearly through translucent materials.

transparent

Light shines through transparent materials such as glass. We can see through them clearly.

Quiz

1 At what speed does light travel?

a) 300 km/sec
b) 3,000 km/sec
c) 30,000 km/sec
d) 300,000 km/sec

2 How does light travel?

a) in straight lines
b) in curved lines
c) in zigzag lines
d) in wavy lines

3 When the sun is low:

a) your shadow is short
b) your shadow is long
c) your shadow is wide
d) your shadow is thin

4 Which materials DON'T let light through?

a) transparent materials
b) translucent materials
c) opaque materials
d) solid materials

5 Which of the following is true?

a) light travels quickest through air
b) light travels quickest through water
c) light travels quickest through glass
d) light travels the same through all materials

6 Convex lenses refract light:

a) outwards
b) inwards
c) upwards
d) downwards

7 Lightning is a type of:

a) reflected light
b) refracted light
c) fluorescent light
d) incandescent light

8 How do fluorescent materials glow?

a) by themselves
b) when they get hot
c) when light shines on them
d) when electricity powers them

9 **Which is NOT a part of the eye?**

a) pupil
b) iris
c) lily
d) retina

10 **Our eyes see:**

a) red, blue and yellow light
b) red, blue and green light
c) red, green and yellow light
d) blue, green and yellow light

ANSWERS 1d, 2a, 3b, 4c, 5a, 6b, 7d, 8c, 9c, 10b

FURTHER INFORMATION

BOOKS

Be a Scientist: Investigating Light by Jacqui Bailey, Wayland

A Question of Science: Why does a mirror show things back to front?
by Anna Claybourne, Wayland

Boom Science: Light by Georgia Amson-Bradshaw, Franklin Watts

Extreme Science: Spectacular Light and Sound by Jon Richards, Wayland

WEBSITES

All about light www.bbc.co.uk/bitesize/topics/zbssgk7/articles/z2s4xfr

Learn and experiment with light! www.optics4kids.org/classroom-activities

Further light experiments to try www.fizzicseducation.com.au/category/150-science-experiments/light-sound-experiments

Find out more and test yourself www.dkfindout.com/uk/science/light

Index